THE BAe Hawk in world wide service
artwork by Jon Freeman

On Target 'Profiles' No 4
BAe Hawk in worldwide service

The BAe Hawk must surely rank as one of the most successful post-war British aircraft designs ever. In service, or on order, with no less than nineteen Air Forces worldwide, the Hawk has made its home in the skies over Europe, the Middle East, India, Africa, the Far East, Australasia and America.

Traditionally, 'advanced trainers', however versatile, tend not to attract as much interest as the more overtly 'warlike' designs, but with its breathtaking performances with the superlative 'Red Arrows' RAF aerobatic team, the type's ongoing development as a very effective ground attack platform and the diverse variety of its colour schemes, the Hawk is destined to be a popular subject with aviation enthusiasts and modellers alike for many more years to come.

On Target 'Profiles'

On Target 'Profiles' are designed to complement your existing camouflage and markings reference material. They are not designed to be the 'last word' on the subject, but to act as sources of inspiration – for aircraft modellers and aviation enthusiasts alike.

All the artwork, in this and all the other titles in this series, (provided by a dedicated group of like-minded aviation enthusiast and aircraft modeller artists), is based upon a mixture of contemporary photographs and information from a variety of sources, to offer as wide a ranging coverage as possible, with good quality, well presented and well-researched colour scheme and markings details for specific aircraft types.

On Target 'Profiles' are also an integral part of a bigger package, comprising these and other modeller-friendly reference books, together with exclusive Model Alliance (UK) decal sheets and conversion sets in 1:144, 1:72 and 1:48 scales.

ON TARGET 'PROFILES'
are published by
THE AVIATION WORKSHOP PUBLICATIONS LTD
Brook Barn, Letcombe Regis, Wantage, Oxfordshire
OX12 9JD United Kingdom
(part of the Model Alliance Group)

Directors:
Gary Madgwick and Neil Robinson
Editorial Consultant Graham Green

Page design and layout by
Mint Ideas
Wath-upon-Dearne, Rotherham

Printed by PHP
Litho Printers Ltd
Barnsley

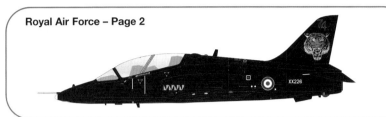
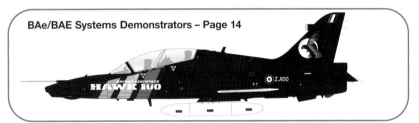

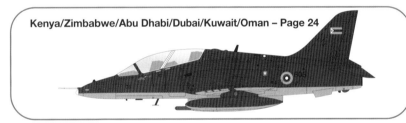

References consulted

'Hawk comes of age' by Peter R March, RAF Benevolent Fund Enterprises, 1995
World Air Power Journal, Volume 22, Autumn 1995, Aeospace Publishing, 1995
'Desert Air Force' by Ian Black, Osprey Publications, 1992
Scale Aircraft Modelling, Vol 23, issue 6, August 2001, Guideline Publications Ltd
Scale Aircraft Modelling, Vol 23, issue 9, November 2001, Guideline Publications Ltd
Scale Aircraft Modelling, Vol 24, issue 2, April 2002, Guideline Publications Ltd
Model Aircraft Monthly, Vol 1, issue 3 March 2002, SAM Publications
Model Aircraft Monthly, Vol 1, issue 6 June 2002, SAM Publications
World Aircraft Information Files Reference File 330
www.airliners.net and http://www.clubhyper.com/reference/hawkdm_4.htm
and with the help, advice and personal photo archives of:-
Gordon G Bartley, Hawk Sales Support, BAE Systems; British Aerospace; Michael Evans; Steve Evans; Graham Green; Steve Mackenzie; Gary Madgwick; Darren Mottram; L/Cdr Gabriel Pincelli; Neil Robinson; and Alexander Sidharta.

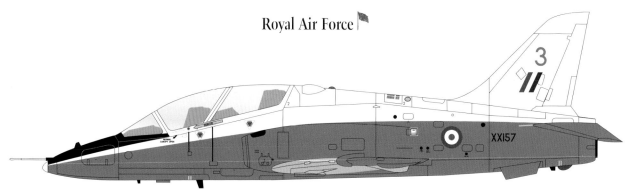

BAe Hawk T Mk 1, XX157, during pre-RAF service trials at Farnborough, circa 1976
Despite being a trials machine, XX157 was finished in the original high visibility 'RAF Trainer' scheme of BS381C: 537 Signal Red fuselage, tailplanes and wing tips with white fuselage spine and fin, and BS381C: 627 Light Aircraft Grey wings. Black anti-glare panel. Red/White/Blue roundels were carried in the usual six positions with the associated fin flash. Black serial number on the rear fuselage and under the wings - reading from the front under the port wing and from the rear under the starboard wing. Note the red 'trials aircraft number' on the fin and the 'short' rear fin fillet.

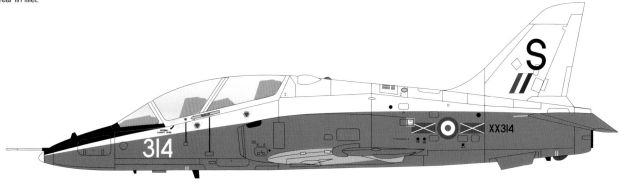

BAe Hawk T Mk 1, XX314/S of No 151 Squadron, RAF Chivenor, circa early 1980s
XX314 was finished in the original standard high visibility 'RAF Trainer' scheme of BS381C: 537 Signal Red fuselage, tailplanes and wing tips with white fuselage spine and fin, and BS381C: 627 Light Aircraft Grey wings. Black anti-glare panel. Red/White/Blue roundels were carried in the usual six positions with the associated fin flash. Black serial number on the rear fuselage and under the wings - reading from the front under the port wing and from the rear under the starboard wing. Note the black aircraft letter on the fin, 'last three' of the serial number in white on the nose and No 151's 'squadron bars' flanking the fuselage roundel. 'Short' rear fin fillet.

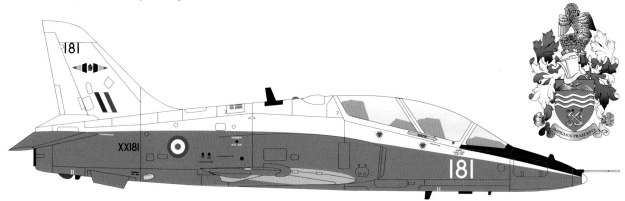

BAe Hawk T Mk 1, XX181 of the Central Flying School, RAF Valley, circa early 1980s
XX181 was finished in the original standard high visibility 'RAF Trainer' scheme of BS381C: 537 Signal Red fuselage, tailplanes and wing tips with white fuselage spine and fin, and BS381C: 627 Light Aircraft Grey wings. Black anti-glare panel. Red/White/Blue roundels were carried in the usual six positions with the associated fin flash. Black serial number on the rear fuselage and under the wings - reading from the front under the port wing and from the rear under the starboard wing. Note the 'last three' of the serial number in black on the fin and in white on the nose. The CFS badge was applied to both sides of the fin (see inset). 'Long' rear fin fillet.

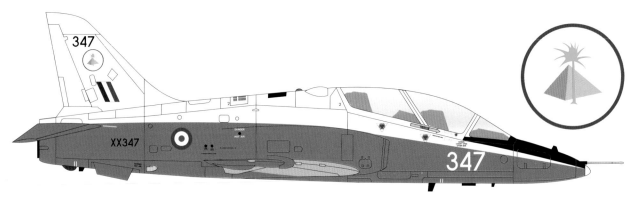

BAe Hawk T Mk 1, XX347 of No 4 Flying Training School, RAF Valley, 1982
XX347 was finished in the original standard high visibility 'RAF Trainer' scheme of BS381C: 537 Signal Red fuselage, tailplanes and wing tips with white fuselage spine and fin, and BS381C: 627 Light Aircraft Grey wings. Black anti-glare panel. Red/White/Blue roundels were carried in the usual six positions with the associated fin flash. Black serial number on the rear fuselage and under the wings - reading from the front under the port wing and from the rear under the starboard wing. Note the 'last three' of the serial number in black on the fin and in white on the nose. The 4 FTS badge was applied to both sides of the fin (see inset). 'Short' rear fin fillet.

BAe Hawk T Mk 1, XX170 of No 4 Flying Training School, RAF Valley, circa 1977

XX170 is illustrated here as she looked when the type first entered RAF service with No 4 FTS, finished in the original standard high visibility 'RAF Trainer' scheme of BS381C: 537 Signal Red fuselage, tailplanes and wing tips with white fuselage spine and fin, and BS381C: 627 Light Aircraft Grey wings. Black anti-glare panel. Red/White/Blue roundels were carried in the usual six positions with the associated fin flash. Black serial number on the rear fuselage and under the wings - reading from the front under the port wing and from the rear under the starboard wing. Note the 'last three' of the serial number on the fin and on the nose - both in black. The original presentation of the 4 FTS badge, within a standard frame, was applied to both sides of the fin (see inset). 'Short' rear fin fillet.

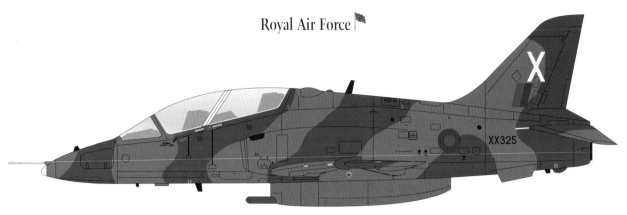

BAe Hawk T Mk 1, XX325/X of No 2 Tactical Weapons Unit, (No 151 'shadow' Squadron), RAF Chivenor, circa 1980s
Overall 'wraparound' tactical scheme of BS381C: 638 Dark Sea Grey and BS381C: 641 Dark Green. Red/Blue roundels were carried in the usual six positions with the associated Red/Blue fin flash. Black serial number on the rear fuselage and under the wings - reading from the front under the port wing and from the rear under the starboard wing. (In early 1981, No 151's St Andrews Cross 'squadron bars' were applied to either side of the fuselage roundels). Note the large white 'X' carried on the fin. 'Long' rear fin fillet.

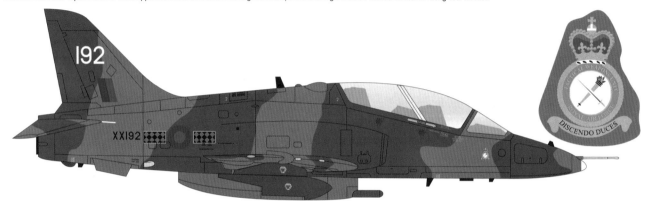

BAe Hawk T Mk 1, XX192 of No 1 Tactical Weapons Unit, (No 234 'shadow' Squadron), RAF Valley, circa 1979
Overall 'wraparound' tactical scheme of BS381C: 638 Dark Sea Grey and BS381C: 641 Dark Green. Red/Blue roundels were carried in the usual six positions with the associated Red/Blue fin flash. Black serial number on the rear fuselage and under the wings. No 234's black and red diamonds 'squadron bars' were applied to either side of the fuselage roundels, with the 'last three' of the serial number on the fin in white. Note the Tactical Weapons Unit badge in a standard frame under the windscreen, (see inset). 'Short' rear fin fillet.

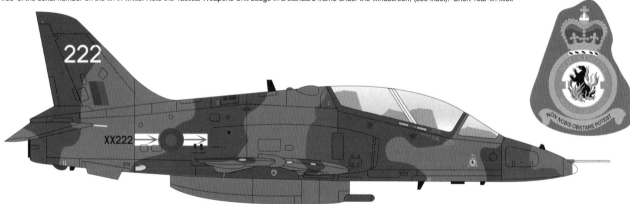

BAe Hawk T Mk 1, XX222 of No 1 Tactical Weapons Unit, (No 79 'shadow' Squadron), RAF Brawdy, 1982
Overall 'wraparound' tactical scheme of BS381C: 638 Dark Sea Grey and BS381C: 641 Dark Green. Red/Blue roundels were carried in the usual six positions with the associated Red/Blue fin flash. Black serial number on the rear fuselage and under the wings. No 79's red arrowhead 'squadron bars' were applied to either side of the fuselage roundels, with the 'last three' of the serial number on the fin in white. Note the No 79 Squadron badge in a standard frame under the windscreen, (see inset). 'Long' rear fin fillet.

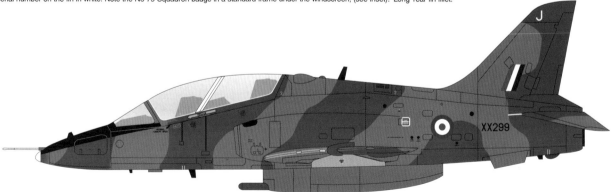

BAe Hawk T Mk 1, XX299, used for camouflage trials, RAF Chivenor, November 1992
In November 1992, the RAF conducted the 'Longview 2 Trials' - air-to-air visibility trials for the Hawk fleet. XX299 was one of the aircraft selected to take part and received a temporary over-all 'wraparound' tactical scheme of Dark Sea Grey and Dark Green over its original Signal Red/White/Light Aircraft Grey trainer scheme. Red/White/Blue roundels, (from the original trainer scheme), were retained and carried in the usual six positions with the associated Red/White/Blue fin flash. Black serial number on the rear fuselage and under the wings. Note the small white 'J' on the fin and the black anti-glare panel infront of the windscreen. Traces of the original trainer scheme Signal Red were visible around the nose. 'Long' rear fin fillet.

BAe Hawk T Mk 1, XX256 of No 2 Tactical Weapons Unit, (No 63 'shadow' Squadron), RAF Chivenor, circa 1981

The Hawk also equipped the RAF's Tactical Weapons Units from the late 1970s and as such, aircraft allocated to the TWUs were finished in camouflage colours. XX325 is illustrated here in the overall 'wraparound' scheme of BS381C: 638 Dark Sea Grey and BS381C: 641 Dark Green. Red/Blue roundels were carried in the usual six positions with the associated Red/Blue fin flash. Units within the TWUs were allocated 'shadow squadron' numbers, (No 1 TWU = 79 and 234 Squadrons; and No 2 TWU = 63 and 151 Squadrons), which were identified by 'squadron bars' on either side of the fuselage roundel - in XX256's case, the No 63 squadron 'bar', comprised of black and yellow checks. Black serial number on the rear fuselage and under the wings - reading from the front under the port wing and from the rear under the starboard wing. The 'last three' of the serial number was applied on the fin in white and the No 63 Squadron badge, within a standard frame, was carried on both sides of the fuselage under the windscreen, (see inset). 'Long' rear fin fillet.

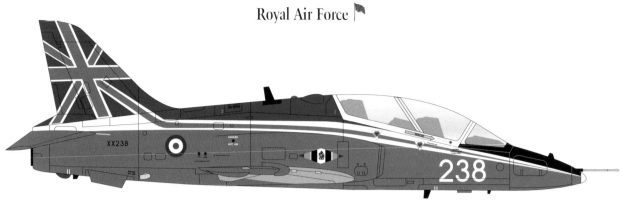

BAe Hawk T Mk 1, XX238 of the Central Flying School, RAF Valley, 1987

The original 'RAF Trainer' scheme was modified in the late-1980s with the white fuselage spine and fin overpainted in BS381C: 110 Roundel Blue with just a white cheatline down the fuselage side. The rest of the scheme remained essentially the same, with Signal Red fuselage, tailplanes and wing tips and Light Aircraft Grey wings. Black anti-glare panel. Red/White/Blue roundels were carried in the usual six positions but the fin flash was replaced by a stylised Union Flag which was applied for the 1987 airshow season. Black serial number on the rear fuselage and under the wings - reading from the front under the port wing and from the rear under the starboard wing. Note the 'last three' of the serial number in white on the nose and the Central Flying School's Coat of Arms insignia on the intake sides, (see inset). 'Long' rear fin fillet.

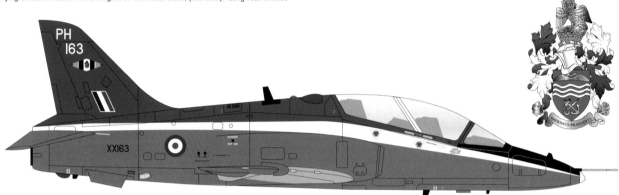

BAe Hawk T Mk 1, XX163 of the Central Flying School, RAF Valley, May 1992

The modified 'RAF Trainer' scheme in Roundel Blue, White, Signal Red and Light Aircraft Grey. Black anti-glare panel. Red/White/Blue roundels were carried in the usual six positions, with the fin flash thinly outlined in white. Black serial number on the rear fuselage and under the wings. Note the 'last three' of the serial number and the code letters 'PH' in white on the fin, together with the Central Flying School's Coat of Arms insignia, (see inset). 'Long' rear fin fillet.

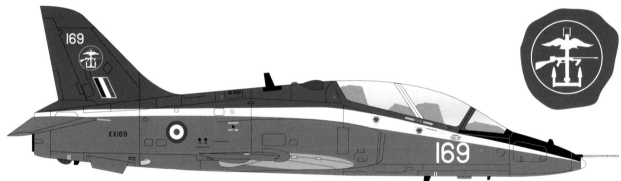

BAe Hawk T Mk 1, XX169 of No 6 Flying Training School, RAF Finningley, circa 1993

Roundel Blue, White, Signal Red and Light Aircraft Grey 'RAF Trainer' scheme with black anti-glare panel. Red/White/Blue roundels in the usual six positions, with the fin flash thinly outlined in white. Black serial number on the rear fuselage and under the wings. Note the 'last three' of the serial number in white on the fin and the forward fuselage, together with No 6 FTS's insignia also in white on the fin, (see inset). 'Long' rear fin fillet.

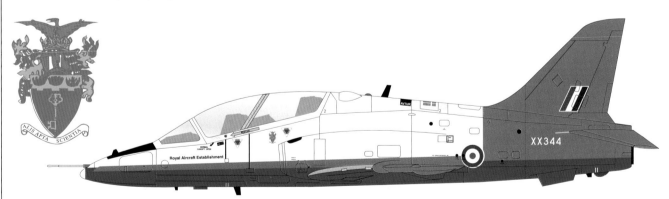

BAe Hawk T Mk 1, XX344 of the Royal Aircraft Establishment, A&AEE, Boscombe Down, circa 1991

XX344 was finished in a variation of the Blue, White, Red and Grey 'RAF Trainer' scheme. The under surfaces of the wings and fuselage were painted in Roundel Blue with a Signal Red cheatline running into the rear fuselage/fin/tailplanes which were also Signal Red. The remainder of the fuselage was white with a black anti-glare panel. The upper surfaces of the wings were Light Aircraft Grey. Red/White/Blue roundels, thinly outlined in white, were in the usual six positions, with the fin flash also thinly outlined in white. White serial number on the rear fuselage. Black serials under the wings. Note the ROYAL AIRCRAFT ESTABLISHMENT legend (in black) on the forward fuselage, together with the RAE crest, (see inset). 'Long' rear fin fillet.

Royal Air Force

BAe Hawk T Mk 1, XX341 of the Empire Test Pilots School, Advanced Systems Training Aircraft (ASTRA), Boscombe Down, 2000

The ETPS was one of the specialised RAF units which operated the Hawk, finished in a modified variation of the Blue, White, Red and Grey 'RAF Trainer' scheme - colloquially known as 'Raspberry Ripple'. The under surfaces of the wings and lower fuselage were painted in Roundel Blue with a Signal Red cheatline running along the fuselage. The upper fuselage sides were white with the fuselage spine and fin, plus the tailplanes, in Signal Red. The upper surfaces of the wings were Light Aircraft Grey and there was a black anti-glare panel infront of the windscreen. Red/White/Blue roundels, thinly outlined in white, were in the usual six positions, with the larger than usual fin flash also thinly outlined in white. The serial number on the rear fuselage was white, whereas the serials under the wings were black. The EMPIRE TEST PILOTS SCHOOL legend and the initials ASTRA, were both in black, on the nose and above the engine intakes. Note the white numeral '1' on the fin. 'Long' rear fin fillet.

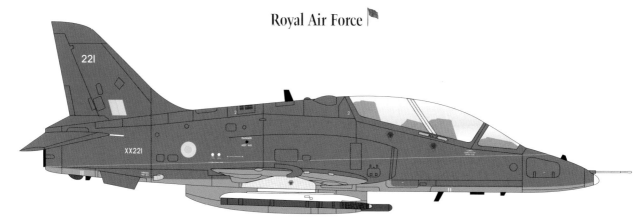

BAe Hawk T Mk 1A, XX221 of No 2 Tactical Weapons Unit, (No 63 'shadow' Squadron), RAF Chivenor, circa late 1983
Several trial camouflage schemes were applied to the Hawk fleet during the 1980s, including this 'Air Defence' scheme applied to four TWU Hawks in late 1983, comprising BS381C: 638 Dark Sea Grey upper surfaces with BS381C: 637 Medium Sea Grey under surfaces. Lo-viz Pale Roundel Red/Pale Roundel Blue roundels were carried in the usual six positions with the associated Pale Roundel Red/Pale Roundel Blue fin flash. The serial number on the rear fuselage was 4 inches high in white - no under wing serials were applied. The 'last three' of the serial number was carried on the fin in white. 'Long' rear fin fillet.

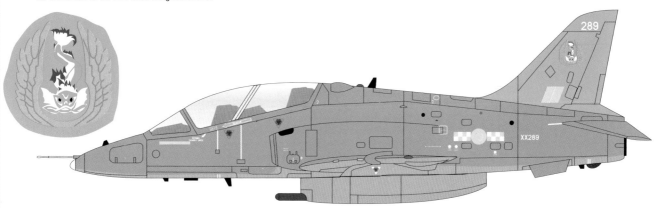

BAe Hawk T Mk 1A, XX289 of No 7 Flying Training School, (No 19 'shadow' Squadron), RAF Chivenor, circa 1992
In April 1992, No 2 TWU was re-designated as No 7 FTS and its two 'shadow' squadrons, (Nos 63 and 151), assumed the identities of the then recently disbanded RAF Germany Phantom squadrons - Nos 19 and 92. Finished in BS381C: 637 Medium Sea Grey upper surfaces with BS381C: 627 Light Aircraft Grey under surfaces, XX289 featured a 'pale blue' fin, (a mix of 50% BS381C: 106 Royal Blue and 50% white), and the 19 Sqn insignia. Lo-viz Pale Roundel Red/Pale Roundel Blue roundels were carried in the usual six positions with the associated Pale Roundel Red/Pale Roundel Blue fin flash. The serial number on the rear fuselage was 4 inches high in white and no under wing serials were applied. The 'last three' of the serial number was carried on the fin in white. 'Long' rear fin fillet.

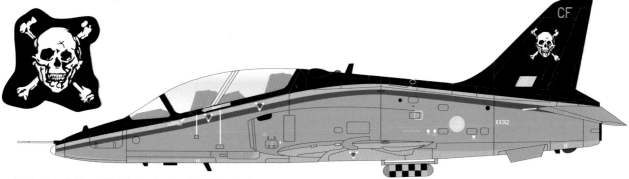

BAe Hawk T Mk 1A, XX312 of No 100 Squadron, RAF Wyton, 1993
XX312 was one of two Hawks painted in this striking scheme for the 75th anniversary of the RAF in 1993. BS381C: 637 Medium Sea Grey upper surfaces with BS381C: 627 Light Aircraft Grey under surfaces. Black fuselage spine and fin with a yellow and blue cheatline. Lo-viz Pale Roundel Red/Pale Roundel Blue roundels were carried in the usual six positions with the associated Pale Roundel Red/Pale Roundel Blue fin flash - in a somewhat truncated form. The serial number on the rear fuselage was 4 inches high in white and no under wing serials were applied. Note the large white 'skull and cross-bones' and Medium Sea Grey codes 'CF' on the fin. 'Long' rear fin fillet.

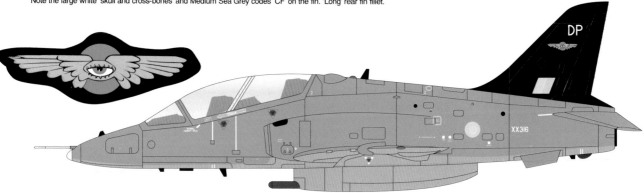

BAe Hawk T Mk 1A, XX316 of No 4 Flying Training School, (No 208 'shadow' Squadron), RAF Valley, circa 1994
BS381C: 637 Medium Sea Grey upper surfaces with BS381C: 627 Light Aircraft Grey under surfaces with a black fin. Lo-viz Pale Roundel Red/Pale Roundel Blue roundels were carried in the usual six positions with the associated Pale Roundel Red/Pale Roundel Blue fin flash. The serial number on the rear fuselage was 4 inches high in white and no under wing serials were applied. No 208's 'winged eye' squadron insignia and white codes 'DP' on fin. 'Long' rear fin fillet.

Royal Air Force

BAe Hawk T Mk 1, XX159 of No 1 Tactical Weapons Unit, (No 79 'shadow' Squadron), RAF Brawdy, 1987

Following the TWU's Dark Sea Grey/Medium Sea Grey scheme trials, (see XX221 opposite), in the mid-1980s, a 'lighter' scheme was eventually decided upon for the Hawk fleet comprising BS381C: 637 Medium Sea Grey upper surfaces with BS381C: 627 Light Aircraft Grey under surfaces. Lo-viz Pale Roundel Red/Pale Roundel Blue roundels were applied in the usual six positions with the associated Pale Roundel Red/Pale Roundel Blue fin flash. The serial number was applied in 4 inch high white characters on the rear fuselage with the 'last three' repeated on the fin. No under wing serials were carried. For the 1987 air display season, XX159 had a BS 381C: 356 Golden Yellow stripe thinly outlined in black, down the fuselage sides and up the fin, with a similarly coloured 'arrowhead' under the wings. The No 79 'shadow' Squadron badge was applied within a standard frame on a white rectangle under the windscreen, (see inset). 'Long' rear fin fillet.

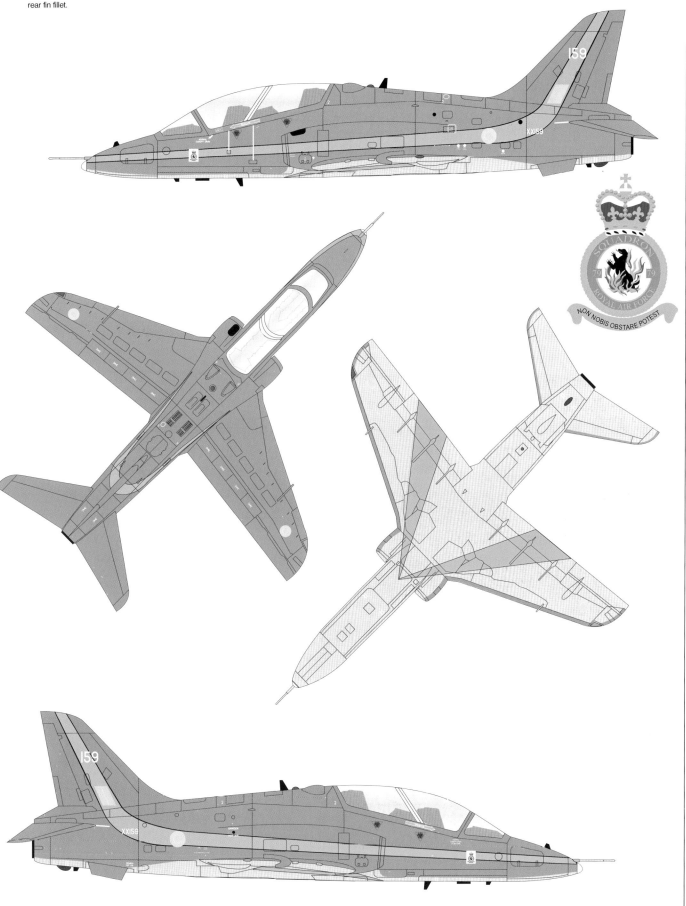

BAe Hawk T Mk 1A, XX162, RAF Centre of Aviation Medicine, RAF Henlow, 1996
Following the 'Longview 2' air-to-air visibility trials In November 1992, (see also XX299 at the bottom of page 4), the RAF finally selected an overall gloss black scheme for its Hawk fleet. Red/White/Blue roundels outlined in white were carried in the usual six positions with the associated Red/White/Blue fin flash also outlined in white. The serial number was applied in white 8 inch high characters on the rear fuselage. No under wing serials were carried. Note the 'RAF CENTRE OF AVIATION MEDICINE' legend in white on the fuselage sides. 'Long' rear fin fillet.

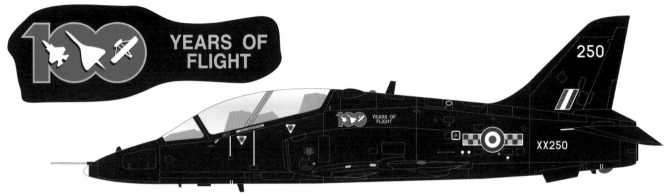

BAe Hawk T Mk 1, XX250, '100 Years of Flight' celebration, No 100 Squadron, RAF St Athan, 2003
Overall gloss black with Red/White/Blue roundels outlined in white in the usual six positions with the associated Red/White/Blue fin flash also outlined in white. The serial number was applied in white 8 inch high characters on the rear fuselage, with the 'last three' repeated on the fin. No 100 Squadron's blue and yellow checks - also thinly outlined in white – appeared on either side of the fuselage roundel, and the '100 Years of Flight' logo was positioned on the fuselage just behind the cockpit. 'Long' rear fin fillet.

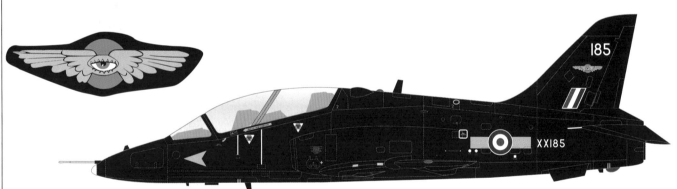

BAe Hawk T Mk 1, XX185, of No 4 Flying Training School, (No 208 'shadow' Squadron), RAF Valley, 2001
Overall gloss black. Red/White/Blue roundels outlined in white were carried in the usual six positions with the associated Red/White/Blue fin flash also outlined in white. The serial number was applied in white, 8 inch high, characters on the rear fuselage, with the 'last three' repeated on the fin. No 208 Squadron's 'winged eye' was positioned on the fin with the blue and yellow squadron bars either side of the fuselage roundel and the chevron under the windscreen. 'Long' rear fin fillet. (see XX316 at the bottom of page 8)

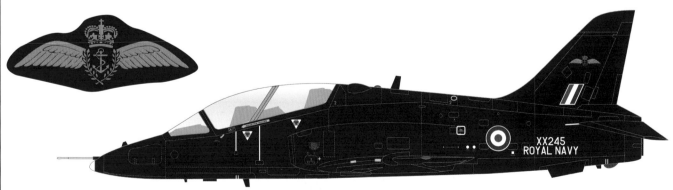

BAe Hawk T Mk 1, XX245, of the Fleet Requirements and Direction Unit (FRADU), Royal Navy, RNAS Yeovilton, 1998
Overall gloss black. Red/White/Blue roundels outlined in white in the usual six positions with the associated Red/White/Blue fin flash also outlined in white. The serial number and ROYAL NAVY in white, 8 inch high, characters on the rear fuselage. Note the FRADU badge on the fin. 'Long' rear fin fillet.

BAe Hawk T Mk 1, XX226, of No 4 Flying Training School, (No 74 'shadow' Squadron), RAF Valley, 2001

XX226 was selected to carry the famous 74 Squadron 'Tigers Head' on its fin. In this 2001 presentation, it will be noted that the Tiger's Head was airbrushed and differs from the earlier 1992 version previously applied to XX226. Overall gloss black with Red/White/Blue roundels outlined in white, carried in the usual six positions but without the fin flash which was presumably over-painted when the Tiger's Head was applied. A yellow, outline only, '74' was positioned above the Tiger's Head on the fin and 'tiger stripe' bars were applied to the intake sides. White 8 inch high serial numbers were carried on the rear fuselage. No under wing serials were carried. 'Long' rear fin fillet.

BAe Hawk T Mk 1, XX172, St Athan Station Flight, RAF St Athan, May 1995

Amongst the most striking schemes carried by Hawks were the 'Welsh Dragon Hawks' illustrated on this and the facing page. The St Athan Station Flight operated a pair of Hawk T Mk 1s, (XX172 shown here and XX184), as 'hacks' to ferry St Athan pilots to and from front line bases. Finished in the then standard Roundel Blue/White/Signal Red/Light Aircraft Grey trainer scheme, XX172 had a black with white outline, Welsh Dragon painted down the full length of the fuselage and up the fin. Red/White/Blue roundels were carried above and below the wings only and the fin flash was thinly outlined in white. Black 4 inch high serial numbers were carried on the rear fuselage and 15 inch high serials under the wings - reading from the front under the port wing and from the rear under the starboard wing. 'Long' rear fin fillet.

BAe Hawk T Mk 1, XX172, St Athan Station Flight, RAF St Athan, 2001

When the standard Hawk scheme was changed to overall glossy black in the mid-1990s, XX172 had its Welsh Dragon re-applied, in a slightly modified form, in red with a thin white outline, but still painted down the full length of the fuselage and up the fin. Red/White/Blue roundels were carried above and below the wings and on the fuselage, the ones on the wings and the fin flash being outlined in white. White 8 inch high serial numbers were carried on the rear fuselage with the 'last three' repeated on the fin over the Dragon's tail. No underwing serials were carried. 'Long' rear fin fillet.

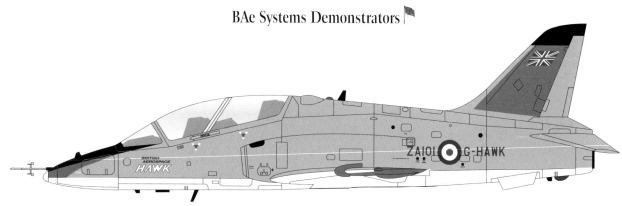

BAe Hawk Mk 50, ZA101/G-HAWK, British Aerospace, 1978-79

In 1978, ZA101/G-HAWK, a basic Hawk 50 airframe, was modified to become the demonstrator for the McDonnell Douglas/BAE VTX/TS contender and toured the USA showing US Navy pilots and key personnel the virtues of the Hawk. Finished in BS381C: 627 Light Aircraft Grey upper surfaces with gloss white undersides, (presumably in an attempt to replicate the US Navy Gull Gray and White scheme), the aircraft featured BS381C: 537 Signal Red panels above and below the wing tips, on the fin and below the black anti-glare panel on the nose. Red/White/Blue roundels were carried in the six usual positions with a Union Flag at the top of the fin. ZA101•G-HAWK appeared in blue on either side of the fuselage roundel and G-HAWK under the port wing, (reading from behind), with the serial number ZA101 repeated under the tailplanes - reading from the front under the port and from the rear under the starboard, again all in blue. The words BRITISH AEROSPACE in blue and HAWK in white outlined in blue, were positioned under the windscreen.

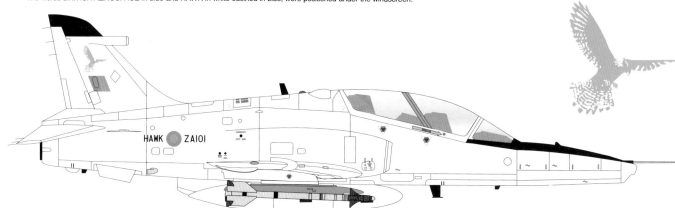

BAe Hawk Mk 100, ZA101/HAWK, British Aerospace, circa 1990

By late 1987, ZA101 had been converted from its basic Hawk 50 airframe with a lengthened and re-shaped nose containing new electronics and sensors. As such it served as the prototype for the Hawk Mk 100 series and first flew in this configuration in October. Overall gloss white with a black anti-glare panel on the nose and black di-electric fin tip fairing. Pale Roundel Red/Pale Roundel Blue roundels were carried in the usual six positions with the Pale Roundel Red/Pale Roundel Blue fin flash applied in a slightly truncated form. Note the early style 'Hawk' emblem in medium grey above the fin flash.

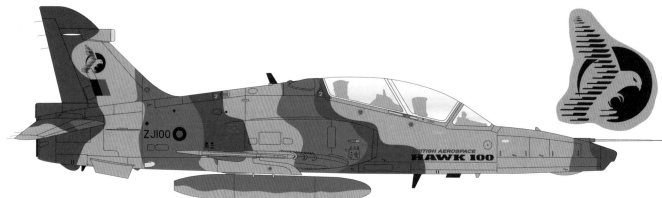

BAe Hawk Mk 100, ZJ100, British Aerospace, 1993-96

ZJ100 is illustrated in its 1993 World Tour configuration, painted in a wraparound camouflage scheme comprising BS 381C: 641 Dark Green, BS 381C: 361 Light Stone and BS 381C: 278 Light Olive Green, to represent a 'South East Asia' style finish. It visited the Middle East, India, the Far East and Australasia and remained in this scheme until 1996. BS381C: 538 Cherry and BS381C: 110 Roundel Blue roundels were carried in the usual six positions with the associated Red/Blue fin flash. A new 'Hawk' design, in Roundel Blue, was carried on the fin. Note the BRITISH AEROSPACE in Roundel Blue and HAWK 100 in black on the nose.

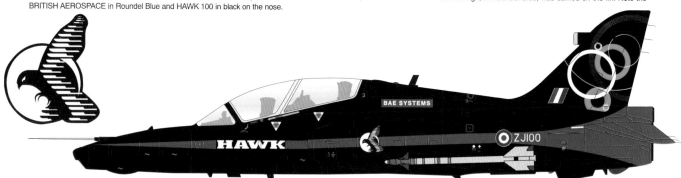

BAe Hawk Mk 100, ZJ100, BAE Systems, 2000-2003

ZJ100 is illustrated here in the Mk 102D configuration, painted in the overall glossy BS381C: 106 Royal Blue with BS381C: 537 Signal Red trim BAE Systems 'Coffee Stain' demonstration scheme, introduced in 2000. 18 inch diameter Red/White/Blue roundels with a 1 inch surround were carried in the usual six positions with the associated Red/White/Blue/white outline fin flash. The 8 inch high white serial number was applied over the Signal Red cheatline with the word HAWK, 'cutting in to' the cheatline under the front canopy. A blue and white 'new' Hawk design was carried mid-fuselage with the controversial 'coffee stain' circles on the fin in white and pale blue. Note the BAE SYSTEMS lettering on a red panel above the intakes.

BAe Systems Demonstrators

BAe Hawk Mk 100, ZJ100, BAe Systems, 1997-1999

ZJ100 was painted in an overall glossy BS381C: 110 Roundel Blue scheme with green, yellow, red and black, (South African national colours), markings on the fuselage and wings for its promotional visit to the Republic of South Africa in 1997. 18 inch diameter Red/White/Blue roundels with a 1 inch surround were carried on the fuselage with the associated Red/White/Blue/white outline fin flash positioned high up on the fin. The 8 inch high white serial number was retained on the rear fuselage with the 'new' Hawk design moved on to the fin, again in South African national colours with the words BRITISH AEROSPACE and HAWK 100, superimposed over the South African national colours stripes on the nose. Note that on the upper/under surfaces of the wings, the red band has no black border to its outer edge.

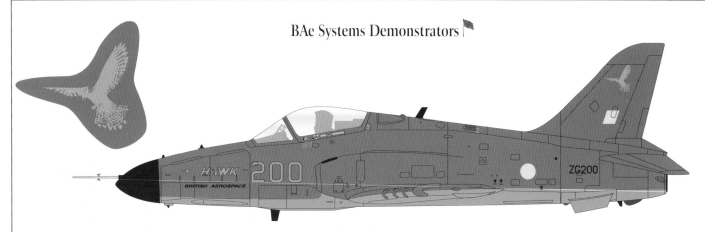

BAe Hawk Mk 200, ZG200, BAe Kingston, May 1986
ZG200 was the prototype Hawk 200, which first flew in May 1986. It was finished in BS381C: 638 Dark Sea Grey upper surfaces over BS381C: 637 Medium Sea Grey. Pale Roundel Red/Pale Roundel Blue roundels were carried in the usual six positions with the associated Pale Roundel Red/Pale Roundel Blue fin flash. The words, BRITISH AEROSPACE in black, and HAWK and the numeral 200, in pale grey outlined in black, were positioned on the nose, with a yellow Hawk design on the fin. Note the black nose cone.

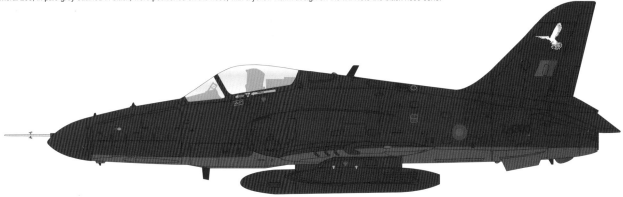

BAe Hawk Mk 200, ZH200, BAe Kingston, April 1987
ZH200 was the second Hawk prototype Hawk 200. It was finished in a two-tone green scheme of BS381C: 285 NATO Green upper surfaces over BS4800: 12B.25 Lichen Green. BS381C: 538 Cherry and BS381C: 110 Roundel Blue roundels were carried in the usual six positions with the associated Red/Blue fin flash. The Hawk design, in white with black detailing, was carried on the fin. Note the nose probe and yaw indicators and the dark green nose cone.

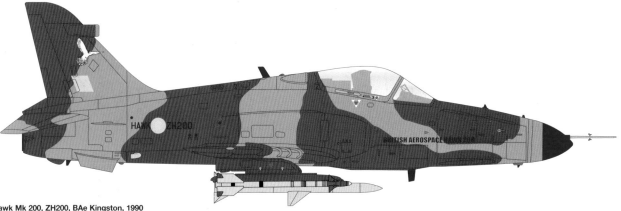

BAe Hawk Mk 200, ZH200, BAe Kingston, 1990
ZH200 was fitted with a fin leading edge Radar Warning Receiver (RWR) and Small Lateral Fuselage Strakes, (Smurfs), in 1989 and re-painted in a wraparound 'desert' scheme, comprising BS381C: 450 Dark Earth and BS381C: 361 Light Stone, to appeal to Middle Eastern customers. Pale Roundel Red/Pale Roundel Blue roundels were carried in the usual six positions with the associated Pale Roundel Red/Pale Roundel Blue fin flash. HAWK•ZH200 was applied to either side of the fuselage roundel, with the words BRITISH AEROSPACE HAWK 200 in black on the nose. The Hawk design, still in white with black detailing, was retained on the fin, as was the nose probe and yaw indicators. Note the black tip to the nose cone.

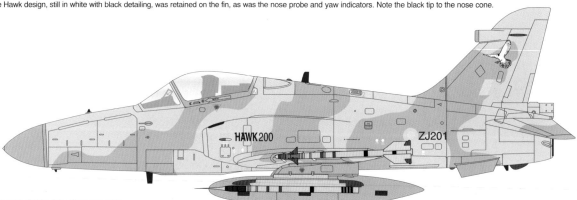

BAe Hawk Mk 200, ZJ201, BAe Kingston, 1994
ZJ201was used as BAe's Radar Development Aircraft, and sported a unique wraparound camouflage scheme of BS381C: 627 Light Aircraft Grey and BS381C: 697 Light Admiralty Grey. Pale Roundel Red/Pale Roundel Blue roundels were in the usual six positions with the associated Pale Roundel Red/Pale Roundel Blue fin flash. The serial number ZJ210 was applied in black 8 inch high characters behind the fuselage roundel with the words HAWK 200 in black on the intake sides. The 'original' Hawk design on the fin comprised of just the black detailing. Note the medium grey nose cone.

BAe Hawk Mk 200, ZJ201, BAe Kingston, 1996

ZJ201was painted in this striking, silver, black and red, 'Maclaren' demonstration scheme and became a very popular attraction at the 1996 airshow season. 12 inch diameter Red/White/Blue roundels were carried in the usual six positions with the associated Red/White/Blue fin flash. The serial number ZJ210 was applied in white 8 inch high characters behind the fuselage roundel with the words HAWK 200 in black and red on the intake sides and BRITISH AEROSPACE DEMONSTRATOR in black and white on the nose. Note the British Aerospace 'arrowhead' logo and the medium grey nose cone. This aircraft was tragically lost in an accident at Bratislava in 1999 whilst sporting a different scheme.

CS-1   SH-60B Seahawk
1:72 Upgrade conversion set for Hasegawa kit   TBA

CS-2   SH-60B Seahawk – 1:72   TBA

CS-3   SH-60F Oceanhawk – 1:72   TBA

CS-4   HH-60H Seahawk
1:72 Conversion set   TBA

CS-5   HH-60J Jayhawk
1:72 scale kit with US Coast Guard decals   £13.50

CS-6   HH-60H Seahawk – 1:72 conversion set
Rescuehawk 2000 (HS Squadrons)   £8.80

CS-7   S-70B/2 Seahawk – 1:72 conversion set
RAN version with standard markings   £13.50

CS-7S   S-70B/2 Seahawk – 1:72 conversion set
RAN version with tiger tail decals   £15.00

CS-8   VH-60N Blackhawk – 1:72 conversion
US President's aircraft including decals   £13.50

CS-9A   S-70A/9 Blackhawk
1:72 RAAF/Australian Army version with decals   £13.50

CS-10   UH-1B/C Huey
1:72 RAN conversion with decals   £6.00

CS-11   UH-1D/H Huey
1:72 RAAF/Australian Army version with decals   £7.15

CS-12   UH-1D/H Huey
1:72 RAAF/Army version includes resin floats   Sold Out

CS-13   US Navy Weapons
1:72 General weapons rails for F-14, A-6, A-4 etc   TBA

CS-14   T-45C Goshawk
1:72 USN improvement set   £8.80

CS-15   CH-47C Chinook
1:72 RAAF original engine filters and
rotor blades (Oz Mods)   £7.15

CS-16   Sea King Mk 51A
1:72 RAN versions with 90s upgrade (no decals)   £8.80

CS-17   SA-365F Daulphin
1:72 French Navy conversion and decals   TBA

CS-18   HH-3F Pelican
1:72 US Coast Guard conversion and decals   £13.50

CS-19   AV-8B + Harrier II
1:72 Conversion set for Airfix/Heller & Italeri kits   £8.80

CS-20   Sea King
1:72 Filter box   £5.00

CS-21   HH-65A Dolphin
1:72 US Coast Guard conversion and decals   £5.00

CS-21   S-70B/2 Seahawk
1:72 RAN Gulf War conversion and decals   £13.50

CS-23   S-2E/G Tracker
1:72 RAN conversion and decals   £17.50

CS-24   SH-2F Seasprite
1:72 RNZN update set and decals sheet   £8.80

CS-25   Boeing 707
1:72 RAAF version and decals high/low viz schemes   £17.50

cs-26   F/A.2 Sea Harrier
1:72 Royal Navy conversion set and decals   £15.00

CS-27   Hawk 127
1:72 RAAF upgrade set and decals for Italeri kit   £8.80

CS-28   MB 339CD
1:72 RNZAF conversion set and decal sheet   £17.50

CS-29   F/A-18 Hornet
1:72 Refuelling probe   £5.00

CS-30   Blackhawk
1:72 HIRSS exhaust kit   £5.00

CS-31   MB 326
1:72 Improvement set   £8.80

CS-32   MB 326
1:72 Dropped wing flaps   £3.85

CS-33   General
1:72 RWR and jammers – mixed set   £3.85

CS-34   Hawk T Mk 1A
1:72 Red Arrows smoke pod   £3.85

CS-35   Sea King
1:72 HAS 5/6 radome   £3.85

CS-36   SH-27 Seasprite
1:72 Fuel tanks   £3.85

CS-37   BAe Hawk 127
1:72 Dropped wing flaps   £3.85

COMING SOON

MAK-7201 Aerospatiale AS 350 Squirrel HT Mk 1
Inlcudes RAF and Armée de Terre decals   TBA

MAK-7202   Aerospatiale AS 350 Twin Squirrel
Inlcudes Queen's Flight decals   TBA

MAK-7203   Aerospatiale AS 555 Fennec
Incl. Danish Army decals and TPW missile system   TBA

MAK-7204   Aerospatiale AS 350B Squirrel
RAN/RAF and DFS including Gulf War modifications   TBA

mak-7205   BAe Sea Harrier F/A.2   **TBA**

MAK-7206   PC-9   **TBA**

MAK-7207   MB 326   **TBA**

MAK-7208   Beech King Air 200   TBA

The BAe Hawk in worldwide service
Available in 1:72 and 1:48 scales – MA72-115 and MA48-115
see order form below

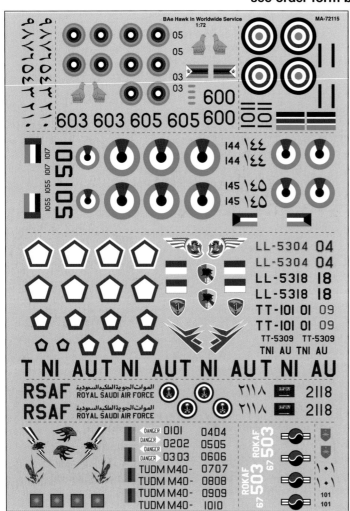

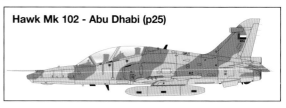

Hawk Mk 102 - Abu Dhabi (p25)

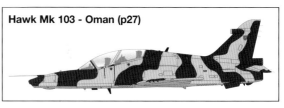

Hawk Mk 103 - Oman (p27)

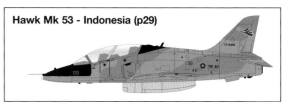

Hawk Mk 53 - Indonesia (p29)

Hawk Mk 65 - Saudi Arabia (p32)

1: Kenya (p24)	6: Oman (p26/27)
2: Zimbabwe (p24)	7: Indonesia (p28/29)
3: Abu Dhabi (p24/25)	8: South Korea (p30)
4: Dubai (p26)	9: Malaysia (p30/31)
5: Kuwait (p26)	10: Saudi Arabia (p32/33)

Canada

BAe Hawk Mk 115/CT-155, 155213 of No 419 Tactical Fighter Squadron, Canadian Air Force, based at Cold Lake, Canada, February 2001
Finished in the overall FS 15044 Glossy Dark Blue scheme, 155213 is one of several CAF CT-155s operated on behalf of the NATO Flying Training Scheme. Canadian 'Maple Leaf' roundels are carried above the port and below the starboard wing and on either side of the rear fuselage, with the fin flash, serial number and NATO FTS badge on the fin. The 'last three' of the serial number is repeated above the starboard and below the port wings and on either side of the nose.

BAe Hawk Mk 127 LIF, A27-21, UP•U of No 79 Squadron, Royal Australian Air Force, RAAF Pearce, September 2003
To celebrate No 79 Squadron's 60th Anniversary, A27-21 had a striking gloss maroon edged in gold, 'tapered flash' painted down the full length of its fuselage and up its fin. The aircraft carried its standard RAAF two-tone grey scheme of overall FS36375 Gray with FS35237 Blue disruptive patches, with FS36375 Gray RAAF roundels on the forward fuselage and above the wings. The FS35237 Blue serial number was re-positioned under the tailplanes and the (World War Two period 79 Squadron) code letters, UP•U, were in gold. Commemorative '1943 - 2003/60 Years' anniversary lettering in yellow was superimposed over a blue numeral 79 on the mid-fuselage area, with No 79 Squadron's phoenix badge, on a white disc edged in gold, just behind the intake. The piéce de resistance, was an airbrushed 'python and flames' artwork on the fin.

BAe Hawk Mk 127 LIF, A27-16, of No 76 Squadron, Royal Australian Air Force, RAAF Williamtown, 2003
Another special RAAF scheme, (designed by artist Darren Mottram), A27-16 featured a black nose, spine and fin – (with red and black trim down the fuselage and under the nose) - over its standard RAAF two-tone grey scheme of overall FS36375 Gray with FS35237 Blue disruptive patches, with red/white/blue roundels on the forward fuselage and FS36375 Gray RAAF roundels above the wings. The FS35237 Blue serial number was positioned on the rear fuselage with a huge black panther on the intake sides. The fin had a red chevron with the No 76 Sqn panther's head badge on a white disc, a large yellow numeral '76' and the Australian national flag.

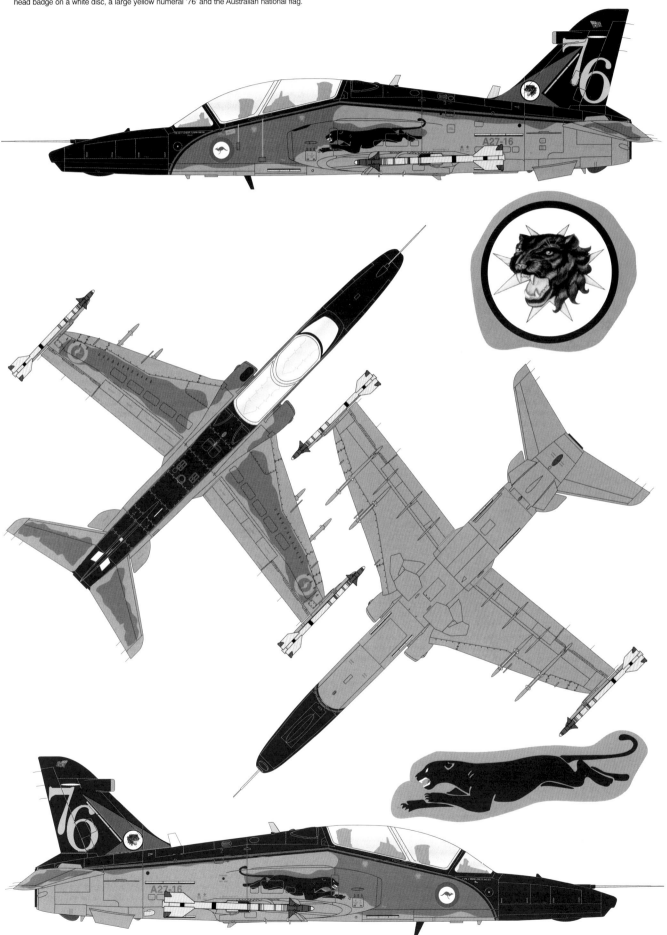

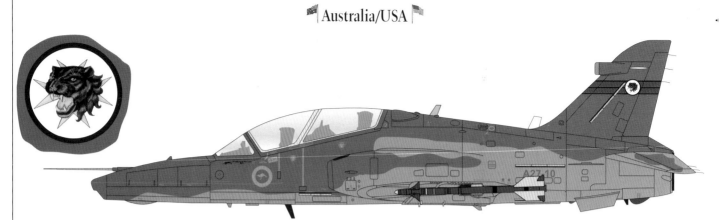

BAe Hawk Mk 127 LIF, A27-10, of No 76 Squadron, Royal Australian Air Force, RAAF Williamtown, 2001, flown by W/Cdr Dave Willcox
Standard RAAF two-tone grey scheme of overall FS36375 Gray with FS35237 Blue disruptive patches, with FS36375 Gray RAAF roundels on the forward fuselage and above the wings. The FS35237 Blue serial number was positioned on the rear fuselage with a black and red band and No 76 Sqn panther's head badge on a white disc, across the chord of the fin.

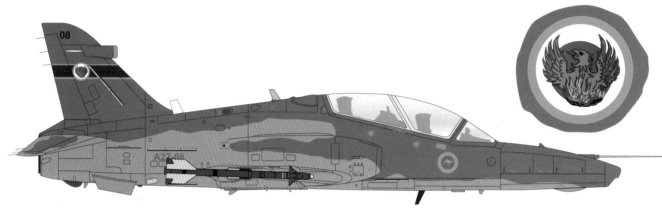

BAe Hawk Mk 127 LIF, A27-08, of No 79 Squadron, Royal Australian Air Force, RAAF Pearce, 2003
Standard RAAF two-tone grey scheme of overall FS36375 Gray with FS35237 Blue disruptive patches, with FS36375 Gray RAAF roundels on the forward fuselage and above the wings. The FS35237 Blue serial number was positioned on the rear fuselage with a maroon band edged in gold and No 79 Sqn phoenix head badge on a white disc, across the chord of the fin. Note the 'last three' of the serial number on the fin tip.

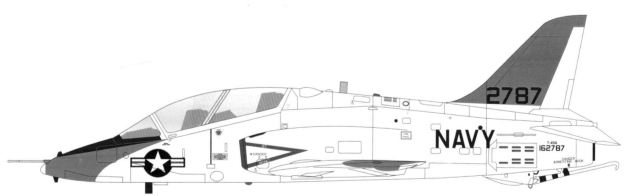

McDonnell Douglas (BAe) T-45 Goshawk prototype, BuAer 162787, circa 1991
The T-45 Goshawk prototype, BuAer 162787 is illustrated here as she initially looked with the original BAe Hawk wing and prior to the numerous changes and modifications she underwent prior to T-45A production standard. Overall Glossy White with FS12197 International Orange nose, fin and wing tip panels. US 'star and bar' on nose and above port/below starboard wings. Note the 'last four' of the BuAer number on the fin tip.

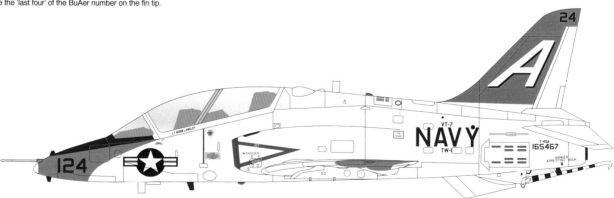

McDonnell Douglas (BAe) T-45A Goshawk, BuAer 165467, 124/A of VT-7 'Eagles', Training Wing 1, United States Navy, based at NAS Meridian, MS, circa 2001
A standard production T-45A Goshawk, BuAer 165467, illustrated in the standard US Navy Goshawk Trainer scheme of Overall Glossy White with FS12197 International Orange nose, fin and wing tip panels. US 'star and bar' on nose and above port/below starboard wings. Note taller fin and large single dorsal fin strake under the rear fuselage. The i/d numerals 124 on the nose and 24 on the fin tip were black with the large white (TW-1) shadow shaded 'A' on the fin.

McDonnell Douglas (BAe) T-45A Goshawk, BuAer 163654, 254/B of VT-21 'Red Hawks', Training Wing 2, United States Navy, based at NAS Kingsville, Texas, circa 1995, flown by L/Cdr Gabriel 'Rage' Pincelli, USM

Although all the T-45s are 'owned' by the US Navy, the USN has the responsibility to train all the US Marine pilots, and a few of the Goshawks carry MARINES titling instead of NAVY, as BuAer 163654, 254/B illustrated here. Overall Glossy White with FS12197 International Orange nose, fin and wing tip panels. US 'star and bar' on nose and above port/below starboard wings. The i/d numerals 254 on the nose and 54 on the fin tip were black with the large black (TW-2) 'B' on the fin. MARINES titling appeared on either side of the rear fuselage and under the port wing tip. Note the taller fin and the large single dorsal fin strake under the rear fuselage, the new slatted wings with 'clipped' tips and larger tailplanes.

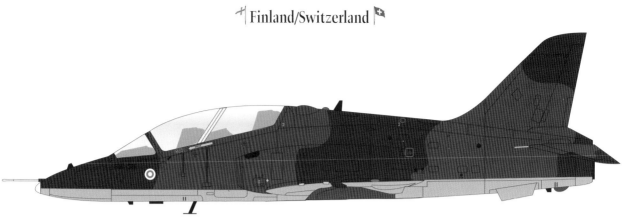

BAe Hawk Mk 51, HW-311 of Ha'vLLv 21, (Fighter Squadron 21), Satakunnan Lennosto, (Satakunnan Wing), Suomen Ilmavoimat, (Finnish Air Force), Tampere/Pirkkala, Finland, 1994
HW-311 is illustrated in the 'interim' camouflage scheme adopted by the Ilmavoimat in the early 1990s, consisting of BS 381C: 437 Very Dark Drab and BS 381C: 222 Light Bronze Green upper surfaces with BS 381C: 627 Light Aircraft Grey undersides. Small, 12 inch diameter, roundels were carried in the usual six positions and the serial number was positioned in small black characters under the windscreen. 'Long' rear fin fillet.

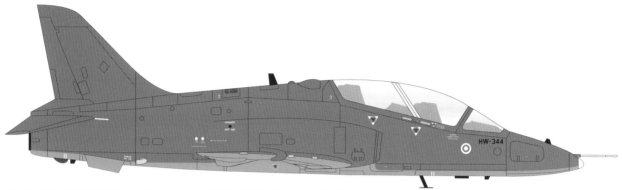

BAe Hawk Mk 51, HW-344 of the Koulutuslentolaiveue, (KouiLLv - Training Squadron), of the Ilmasotakoulu, (Air Academy), Suomen Ilmavoimat, (Finnish Air Force), Kauhava, Finland, 1994
In late the 1990s, Finland adopted a 'grey' scheme for its Hawk fleet, comprising BS 381C: 638 Dark Sea Grey upper surfaces with BS 381C: 637 Medium Sea Grey under surfaces. Small, 12 inch diameter, roundels were carried in the usual six positions and the serial number was positioned in small black characters under the windscreen. 'Long' rear fin fillet.

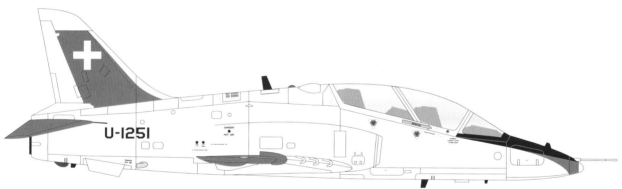

BAe Hawk Mk 66, U-1251 of Fliegerschule 1, Kommando der Flieger (Swiss Air Force), Emmen, 1990
The first Swiss Hawk, U-1251 was initially finished in an overall white scheme with BS381C: 537 Signal Red nose flash (with black anti-glare panel), fin, tailplanes and wing tips. The white Swiss cross marking was carried in the usual six positions on the Signal Red areas. The black serial number was carried on the rear fuselage. 'Long' rear fin fillet.

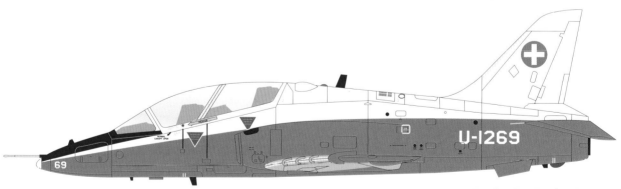

BAe Hawk Mk 66, U-1269 of Fliegerschule 1, Kommando der Flieger (Swiss Air Force), Emmen, 1992
The Swiss Air Force adopted a finish identical to the original high visibility 'RAF Trainer' scheme for its Hawk fleet, comprising BS381C: 537 Signal Red fuselage, (with black anti-glare panel), tailplanes and wing tips with white fuselage spine and fin, and BS381C: 627 Light Aircraft Grey wings. The white Swiss cross marking was carried in the usual six positions on a Signal Red disc on the fin and the Signal Red areas of the wings. The white serial number was carried on the rear fuselage. Note the 'long' rear fin fillet.

✠ Finland

BAe Hawk Mk 51, HW-338 of Ha'vLLv 21, (Fighter Squadron 21), Satakunnan Lennosto, (Satakunnan Wing), Suomen Ilmavoimat, (Finnish Air Force), Pori, Finland, mid-1986
For a brief period in mid-1986, Hawks comprised the first line defence of the south-west of the country until more SAAB Drakens were taken into Ilmavoimat service. HW-338 is illustrated whilst based at Pori in the Air Defence role, sporting the initial delivery camouflage scheme consisting of BS 381C: 437 Very Dark Drab and BS 381C: 222 Light Bronze Green upper surfaces with BS 381C: 627 Light Aircraft Grey undersides . Standard 18 inch diameter, roundels were carried in the usual six positions and the serial number was positioned in large black characters on the rear fuselage. 'Long' rear fin fillet.

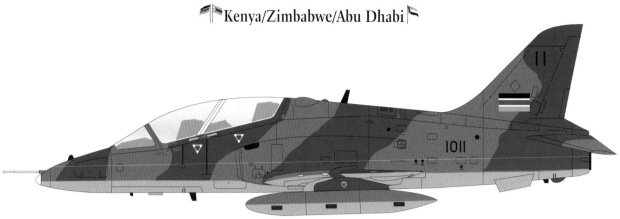

BAe Hawk Mk 52, 1011, Kenya Air Force, Nanyuki, 1982
Kenya became the Hawk's first export recipient when the first of its twelve Mk 52s was delivered in April 1980. All twelve aircraft were finished in BS381C: 638 Dark Sea Grey and BS381C: 641 Dark Green upper surfaces with BS 381C: 627 Light Aircraft Grey undersides. Kenyan Air Force green/white/red/white/black roundels were carried above and below the wings with a horizontally striped fin flash. A black serial number was carried on the rear fuselage, the 'last two' of which was repeated on the fin. 'Long' rear fin fillet.

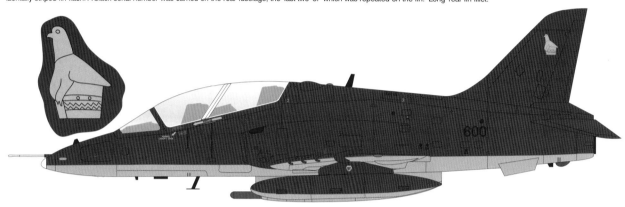

BAe Hawk Mk 60, 600, No 2 Squadron, Air Force of Zimbabwe, Gwelo, July 1982
Zimbabwe's Hawks were finished in ICI 407-1913 Matt Green and ICI 407-1914 Matt Brown upper surfaces with BS 381C: 627 Light Aircraft Grey undersides. Initial delivery aircraft carried no national markings other than the yellow 'bird on a crown' on the fin. A black serial number was carried on the rear fuselage. This particular Hawk had to be returned to the UK in the autumn of 1982 for an extensive re-build following damage caused by sabotage. 'Long' rear fin fillet.

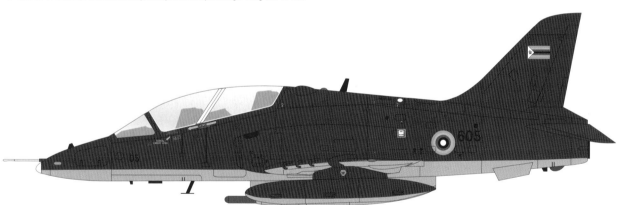

BAe Hawk Mk 60, 605, No 2 Squadron, Air Force of Zimbabwe, Gwelo, mid-1980s
Still finished finished in ICI 407-1913 Matt Green and ICI 407-1914 Matt Brown upper surfaces with BS 381C: 627 Light Aircraft Grey undersides, Zimbabwe's Hawk fleet adopted new markings in the mid-1980s. Roundels comprising the Zimbabwe national colours of white/black/red/yellow/green were carried on the upper surfaces of the wings and on the fuselage, with a horizontally striped fin flash. The black serial number was carried on the rear fuselage with the 'last two' repeated in smaller characters on the nose. 'Long' rear fin fillet.

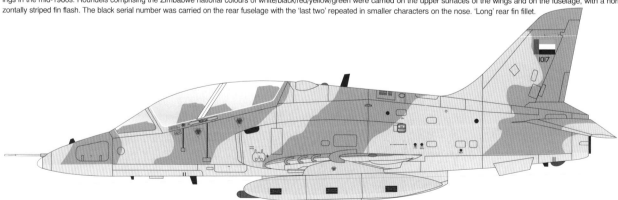

BAe Hawk Mk 63C, 1017, Flying Training School, Abu Dhabi Air Force, United Arab Emirates, Maqatra, 1995
1017 was one of four Mk 63Cs delivered in early 1995, and featured the seven-station combat wing. Finished in BS 381C: 361 Light Stone and BS 381C: 388 Beige upper surfaces the under surfaces were finished in ICI F407-1915 Light Blue-grey which is similar to FS35526. Black/white/green/red United Arab Emirates roundels were carried above and below the wings, with the similarly coloured UAE fin flash. A small black serial number was carried on the fin under the fin flash. 'Long' rear fin fillet.

Abu Dhabi

BAe Hawk Mk 102, 1055, Flying Training School, Khalif Bin Zayed Air College, Abu Dhabi Air Force, United Arab Emirates, Maqatra, 1994

Abu Dhabi was the first export customer for the Hawk 100 design and purchased eighteen examples in 1993, finished in BS 381C: 361 Light Stone and BS 381C: 388 Beige upper surfaces with ICI F407-1915 Light Blue-grey (similar to FS35526) under surfaces. Red/green/white/black United Arab Emirates roundels were only carried above and below the wings initially, with fuselage roundels being added at a later date. A red/green/white/black UAE fin flash was positioned on the fin below which was a small black serial number. 'Long' rear fin fillet.

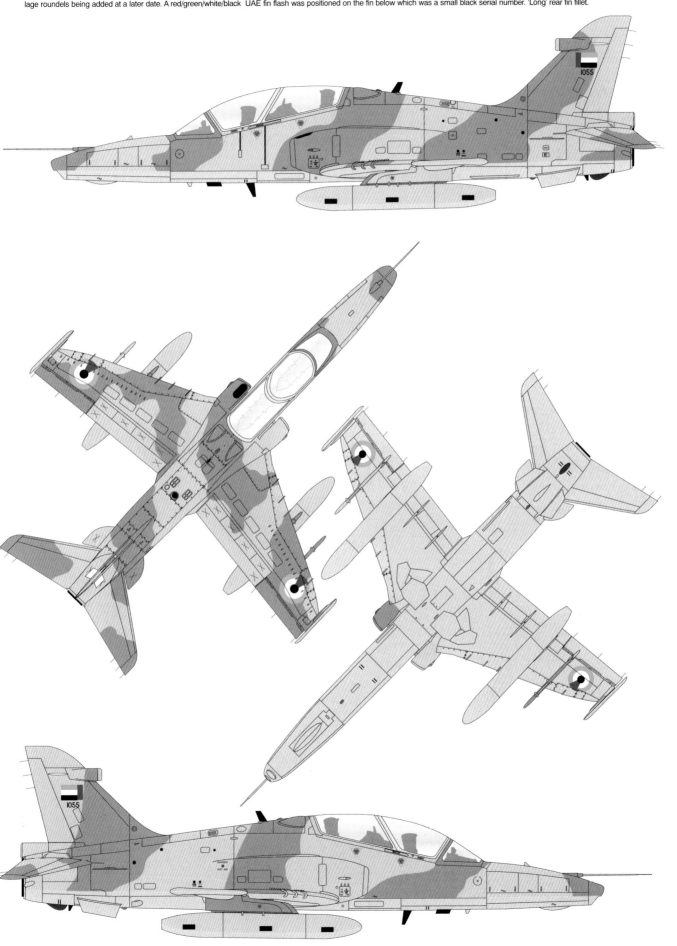

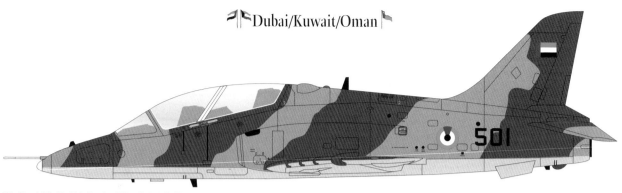

BAe Hawk Mk 61, 501, Combat Wing, Dubai Air Wing, United Arab Emirates, Mindhat, 1984
Dubai ordered eight Mk 61s which were delivered in 1983, plus a further attrition replacement airframe in 1988. All were finished in BS 381C: 450 Dark Earth and BS 381C: 410 Light Brown upper surfaces with ICI F407-1915 Light Blue-grey (similar to FS35526) under surfaces. Red/green/white/black United Arab Emirates roundels were carried in all six positions - above/below the wings and on the fuselage sides - with a red/green/white/black UAE fin flash on the fin. A large black serial number appeared on the rear fuselage which was repeated on some aircraft in much smaller Arabic numerals on the nose. 'Long' rear fin fillet.

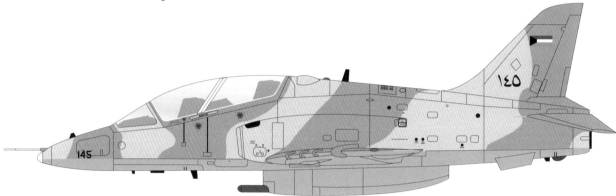

BAe Hawk Mk 64, 145, No 12 Squadron, Al Quwwat al Jawwiya al Kuwaitiya, (Kuwait Air Force), Ahmed al Jaber, circa 1986
The Kuwait Air Force ordered twelve Mk 64s in late 1983. The initial delivery scheme comprised BS 381C: 361 Light Stone and BS 381C: 388 Beige upper surfaces with BS 381C: 627 Light Aircraft Grey under surfaces. No national markings were carried other than a black/red/white/green fin flash on the fin. A black serial number in Arabic numerals was positioned on the fin with smaller anglicised numerals on the nose. 'Long' rear fin fillet.

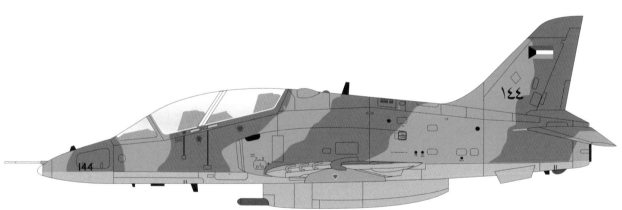

BAe Hawk Mk 64, 144, No 12 Squadron, Al Quwwat al Jawwiya al Kuwaitiya, (Kuwait Air Force), Ahmed al Jaber, circa 1998
By the early 1990s the Kuwait Air Force had revised its Hawk fleet colour scheme to BS 381C: 638 Dark Sea Grey and BS 381C: 637 Medium Sea Grey upper surfaces with BS 381C: 627 Light Aircraft Grey under surfaces. Black/red/white/green roundels were applied to the under surfaces of the wings only with a matching fin flash on the fin. A black serial number in Arabic numerals was positioned on the fin with smaller anglicised numerals on the nose. 'Long' rear fin fillet.

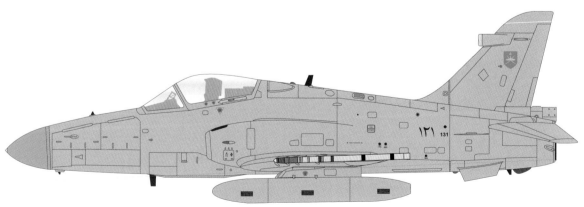

BAe Hawk Mk 203, 131, No 6 Squadron, Al Quwwat al Jawwiya al Oman, (Royal Air Force of Oman), Masirah, circa 1995
Oman was the launch export customer for the single-seater Mk 203, ordering twelve in 1990. Finished in an overall BS 381C: 627 Light Aircraft Grey scheme with a medium grey nose radome, the only national markings appeared on the fin in the form of the blue shield with yellow detail. A black serial number in Arabic numerals with smaller anglicised numerals next to it were positioned on the rear fuselage.

Oman

BAe Hawk Mk 103, 101, No 6 Squadron, Al Quwwat al Jawwiya al Oman, (Royal Air Force of Oman), Masirah, circa mid-2000
To provide lead-in training for the Hawk 203 fleet, Oman ordered four twin-seater Mk 103s fitted with wing tip AIM-9 Sidewinder rails. Finished in a BS 381C: 450 Dark Earth and BS 381C: 388 Beige upper surface 'desert' scheme with BS 381C: 627 Light Aircraft Grey under surfaces, the only national markings appeared on the fin in the form of the blue shield with yellow detail. A black serial number in Arabic numerals with smaller anglicised numerals next to it were positioned on the rear fuselage.

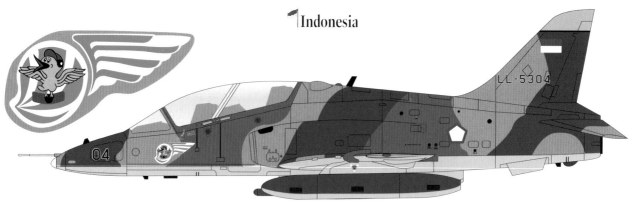

BAe Hawk Mk 53, LL-5304, No 10 Squadron, No 1 Training Wing, Tentara Nasional Indonesia-Angkatan Udara (Indonesian Armed Forces - Air Force), Adisutjipto, Jogjakarta, 1980
Indonesia became the third BAe Hawk export customer when it initially ordered eight Mk 53s in 1978. Assigned to the weapons training role, the aircraft were delivered in a 'South East Asian' scheme of Dark Green FS 34079, Medium Green FS 34079 and Tan FS30219 upper surfaces with Gray FS 36622 under surfaces. Red/white Air Force 'hexagon' national markings appeared in the six usual positions with the red/white horizontally striped fin flash on the fin. The black serial number on the fin was outlined in yellow with the 'last two' repeated on the nose. The wings and fin sported yellow tips. Note the No 1 Training Wing insignia on the nose.

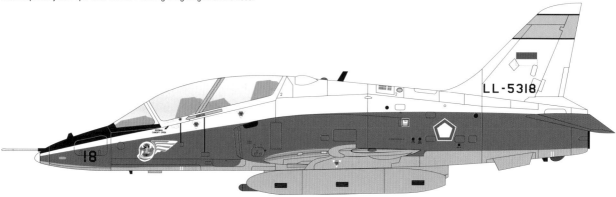

BAe Hawk Mk 53, LL-5318, Skwadron Latih Lanjut 103, (103 Advanced Flying Squadron), Tentara Nasional Indonesia-Angkatan Udara (Indonesian Armed Forces - Air Force), Iswahyudi/(Madiun), 1984
Follow-on orders in 1981 and 1982 resulted in a further twelve Mk 53s being delivered, the last three, LL-5318, LL-5319 and LL-5320, sporting an RAF-style trainer scheme in US Federal Standard shades of FS 11136 Red, white and FS 36622 Gray with BS 381C: 356 Yellow fin stripe and wing tips thinly bordered in black. Red/white Air Force 'hexagon' national markings appeared in the six usual positions with the ones on the fuselage thinly outlined in white. The red/white horizontally striped fin flash on the fin had the lower red rectangle thinly outlined in red. The black serial number on the fin had the 'last two' repeated on the nose. No 10 Squadron, No 1 Training Wing, was re-named No 103 Advanced Flying Squadron in 1981 but retained the No 1 Training Wing insignia on the nose.

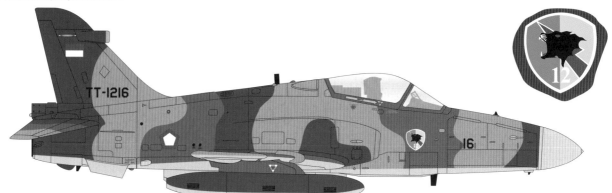

BAe Hawk Mk 209, TT-1216, No 12 Squadron, Tentara Nasional Indonesia-Angkatan Udara (Indonesian Armed Forces - Air Force), Pekanbaru, 1997
An initial batch of sixteen 200 series Hawks, with Westinghouse APG-66 radar, were delivered to Indonesia in 1993 with another batch in 1996. All were delivered in the 'South East Asian' scheme of Dark Green FS 34079, Medium Green FS 34079 and Tan FS30219 upper surfaces with Gray FS 36622 under surfaces. Red/white Air Force 'hexagon' national markings appeared in the six usual positions with the red/white horizontally striped fin flash on the fin. The black serial number on the fin had the 'last two' repeated on the nose. Note the No 12 Squadron insignia on the nose.

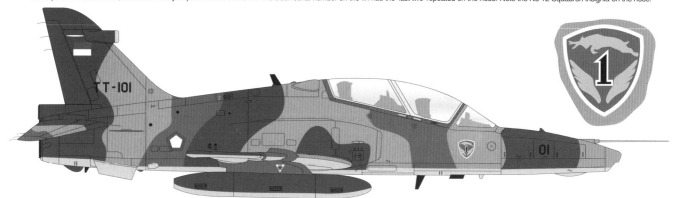

BAe Hawk Mk 209, TT-101, No 1 Squadron, Tentara Nasional Indonesia-Angkatan Udara (Indonesian Armed Forces - Air Force), Pontianak, 2001
Ordered in 1993, the TNI-AU took delivery of eight Adour 871-powered Mk 109s in 1996. These aircraft were also finished in the 'South East Asian' scheme of Dark Green FS 34079, Medium Green FS 34079 and Tan FS30219 upper surfaces with Gray FS 36622 under surfaces. Red/white Air Force 'hexagon' national markings appeared in the six usual positions with the red/white horizontally striped fin flash on the fin. The black serial number on the fin had the 'last two' repeated on the nose. Note the No 1 Squadron insignia on the nose.

BAe Hawk Mk 208, M40-32, No 9 Squadron, Tentara Udara Diraja Malaysia, (Malaysian Air Force), Kuantan, 2000
Overall BS 381C: 637 Medium Sea Grey scheme with the blue, black and yellow Malaysian national markings above the port and below the starboard wings and on either side of the fuselage, with an accompanying fin flash. The TUDM legend and the serial number are positioned above and below the formation light strip on the fuselage with TUDM above the starboard and below the port wings. Note the No 9 Golden Eagle Squadron badge with red lightning flashes on the fin and the lighter grey nose radome.

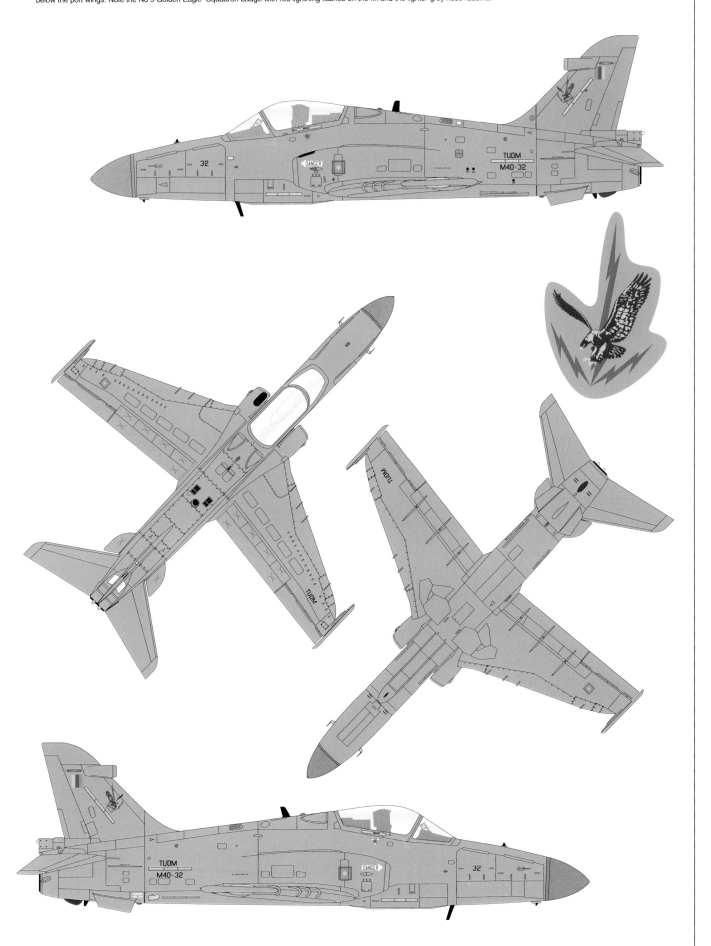

BAe Hawk Mk 65, 2118, No 21 Squadron, Al Quwwat al Jawwiya as Sa'udiya, (Royal Saudi Air Force), Riyadh Air Academy, circa 1991

As part of Phase 1 of the Al Yamamah Project, the Royal Saudi Air Force ordered thirty Hawk Mk 65s which were delivered in two batches, the first between October 1987/January 1988 and the second in February 1988. All were finished in this striking wraparound camouflage scheme of BS 381C: 450 Dark Earth, BS 381C: 641 Dark Green and BS 381C: 388 Beige. The green and white RSAF roundels were carried above the port and below the starboard wings and on either side of the fuselage with the 'fin flash' on the fin. The aircraft's serial number, in both arabic and anglicised characters, was also positioned on the fin in black with the ROYAL SAUDI AIR FORCE legend, again in both arabic and anglicised script, on the nose in green and RSAF above the starboard and below the port wings again in green. The RSAF used their Hawks in the ground attack role during the 1991 Gulf War and also in the Point Air Defence role, armed with AIM-9L Sidewinders.